MW01283494

Štěpánka Sekaninová
Linh Dao

DIARY
OF A
BEE

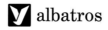albatros

SPRING IN THE MEADOW

In a sunlit meadow near a forest, there is a beehive. It's humming and buzzing with busy little bees flying off and returning from their journeys for water, pollen, and sweet nectar from flowers. Would you like to take a look inside their kingdom? Come on then! Tread softly and let's quietly observe what's happening in the hive.

JUST BORN

Hello,
I'm Matilda.

Oh, how I enjoyed being a wee little larva! The bees fed me and I just lay there in my cell, eating and sleeping for days on end. After that, they sealed the cell and I turned into a prepupa and later a pupa. After that, I slowly became a bee.

egg

larva

bigger larva

prepupa

pupa

It only took 21 days for me to be born!

WELCOME TO OUR HIVE

This is our hive! It's so beautiful and it smells just wonderful! Want to take a look around?

Our hive consists of wax honeycombs made up of cells shaped like six-sided hexagons. We ordinary workers develop in the smallest cells, while drones have larger ones.

The royal chamber – the cell of the queen bee – looks completely different. It's only proper that the queen has a grander chamber, as befits her status.

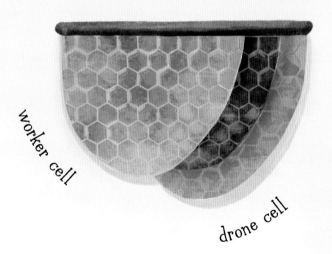

worker cell

drone cell

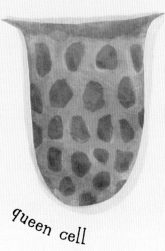

queen cell

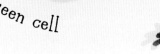

Me with mother and Thomas

This is me next to the queen, my mother. A drone named
Thomas is also here. He was born on the same day as me.
Drones are boy bees. It takes them 24 days to develop
in their cells, whereas queens emerge in only 16 days.

DAY 1 IN THE HIVE

Let me tell you, after I hatched I was quite the mess – very weak and confused. However, the older bees rushed to my aid at once and fed me sweet honey and pollen, which boosted my strength.

I love cleaning.

DAY 2 IN THE HIVE

After I was up and about, there was no time to waste. As a worker bee, part of my job is to clean, so I started tidying up the cells. I make them nice and clean to prepare them for new eggs.

DAY 3 IN THE HIVE

Hooray! Today I got a new job! I'm a feeder. I can now feed myself honey and pollen. And, what's more, I can make honey in my honey sac. So now I can feed others.

I also love feeding.

DAY 4 IN THE HIVE

I feed and feed and do nothing but feed. I have only a few seconds for each larva! Why oh why wasn't I born a drone! How is it that Thomas does nothing? Apparently, he needs to rest before he flies off on his wedding flight. It was also nice to take a peek outside for the first time today.

DAY 6 IN THE HIVE

I feed others all day long, and I also pack pollen brought by forager bees into the wax cells. I then add a special goo from my body that makes the pollen start to ferment (meaning it's preserved to last a long time). In the afternoon, I looked outside for the second time. There is nothing so lovely as a sunlit meadow!

The world is
shiny and fragrant.
I can't wait to
go out.

DAY 7 IN THE HIVE

I can now make the special milk that is best for feeding newly hatched bees, drones, and even the queen herself. I'm now a nurse bee. I fed my mother today. She's laying eggs and needs to eat a lot.

DAY 8 IN THE HIVE

Today I celebrated the eighth day of my life. I'm no longer on nursing duty, as I have a new task. I wait by the entrance to the hive and take the nectar brought by the forager bees. I then store it in the honeycomb and seal the cells when they're full. I talk a lot with everyone, including Thomas. It's only six days before his wedding flight.

A little more wax and the new chamber is done.

DAY 12 IN THE HIVE

As of today, my body is able to produce wax. So I'm helping to build new cells. I'm a builder. I heard that the wedding flight of the young queen and the drones is only two days away. That's why Thomas is strutting proudly around the hive with his nose in the air.

DAY 14 IN THE HIVE

The big day has arrived! It's the day of the wedding flight. Thomas is the youngest of all the drones, at only 14 days old, which is the minimum age to take part. They say that those drones who succeed in mating with the queen will not return to the hive. Having fulfilled their task, they will die. The others will fly back to us. I sure do hope Thomas comes back – I like him.

DAY 15 IN THE HIVE

Hooray, Thomas is back! I'm so happy, but he doesn't want to talk. He's disappointed because he couldn't finish his task. Meanwhile, there was a crack in the hive that I had to fill. I must say I made a fine job of it. I think I have great talent as a builder.

We'll protect you.

DAY 18 IN THE HIVE

Today I am exactly 18 days old. I got a big honey cake with 18 candles on it. I've been so looking forward to it. From now on, I'm going to stand guard to make sure the hive is protected.

DAY 19 IN THE HIVE

Oh, what a day I've had! A hungry bee broke into the hive and tried to help himself to our supplies. I fought bravely with the burglar and chased him away. I really did myself proud as a guard!

DAY 21 IN THE HIVE

It's a sad day for all of us. One of
the oldest bees in our hive died.
Her wings were completely worn
out from all the flying she'd done
in her life. To pay our last respects,
we carried her out of the hive
and returned her to nature.

DAY 22 IN THE HIVE

I'm now no longer a youngster, so I'm starting my duties as a forager bee. I'll be flying missions outside the hive. I'm looking forward to meadows and blue skies. But many foragers never return from their journeys. They get swallowed by birds or trampled by humans. It's a dangerous business being a forager.

DAY 22 IN THE HIVE (LATER THAT NIGHT)

I'm tired and my wings are aching, but it was well worth it. I flew out of the hive and back six times! Fortunately, I didn't have to fly very far, as the scout bee had told us that there was a cherry tree in blossom only one mile away. I immediately fell in love with cherry blossoms. After I've pollinated the whole tree, I'm going to find another cherry tree. We bees stay loyal to the species of plants we choose.

OUR BEE LANGUAGE

This is how we bees talk to each other: by dancing. When we turn in a circle, it means there's a source of food nearby. When we do a figure-eight dance, we're talking about where the food is and how long it takes to fly there.

DAY 23 IN THE HIVE

I love all the many different colors of flowers. They're amazing! We bees only see shades of blue, violet, and ultraviolet. Catherine, a wise, elderly bee who remembers a lot, once told us that humans can see other colors too – yellows, greens, reds, oranges, and who knows what else! I can't imagine it.

DAY 24 IN THE HIVE

Once again, I flew six times and collected 24 million grains of pollen. Our mother, the queen, told me I'm one of our most hard-working bees.

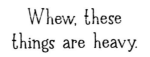

Whew, these things are heavy.

DAY 25 IN THE HIVE

Thomas is getting more bored with every day that goes by. He has no work to do. He just lazes around the hive being fed honey. He's no fun anymore. But at least he helps to warm the hive when it's cold. And on warmer days, he also helps cool it with his wings.

Shhh, don't disturb her, she's still sleeping.

DAY 26 IN THE HIVE

Our hive is getting to be a bit cramped.
There's a new queen developing in the queen
cell, so our old queen and her retinue of
workers and scouts are going to swarm and
start a new colony. That's why they spend all
day taking honey from the honeycombs and
filling their honey sacs – they need supplies.
One thing is for sure, I'm going to miss my mother.

DAY 31 IN THE HIVE

There's plenty of space here in the hive again ... and a new queen too. Having only recently hatched, she's still young, but she's also clever and kind, just like our former queen.

our new queen

DAY 35 IN THE HIVE

I love how excited the young forager bees are about the world. They're just like I used to be. It aches my wings to think about the amount of water, pollen, and nectar I've gathered. At one time, I would spend two whole hours outside. Today I'm glad to be back after a few minutes. Oh well, I have my 155th flight ahead of me. I'll give my wings a little massage and then off I go!

Thomas here, bidding you farewell.

DAY 37 IN THE HIVE

I'm afraid our Matilda is no longer with us in the hive. Two days ago, she flew off to forage and never came back. Such is life! That's just the way it goes with us bees. Don't be sad, though, kids. There are plenty of new young Matildas swarming around me. And since autumn has arrived, we old drones have to make space for them.

AND SPRING AGAIN

After each winter, spring is sure to follow, and in spring the beehives come to life again. They bustle with activity to the sounds of buzzing and humming. Once again, new workers and drones are born in every hive, just like in ours. Why don't you take a look? Matilda and Thomas are already impatiently beckoning ...

DIARY OF A BEE

© B4U Publishing for Albatros,
an imprint of Albatros Media Group, 2025
5. května 1746/22, Prague 4, Czech Republic
Author: Štěpánka Sekaninová
Illustrator: Linh Dao
Translator: Mark Worthington
Editor: Scott Alexander Jones

Printed in China by Leo Paper Group Ltd.

www.albatrosbooks.com

All rights reserved.
Reproduction of any content is strictly prohibited
without the written permission of the rights holders.

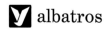